*The Dragonfly Will Be
the Messiah*

The Dragonfly Will Be the Messiah

MASANOBU FUKUOKA

Translated by Larry Korn

PENGUIN BOOKS — GREEN IDEAS

PENGUIN BOOKS

UK | USA | Canada | Ireland | Australia
India | New Zealand | South Africa

Penguin Books is part of the Penguin Random House group of companies
whose addresses can be found at global.penguinrandomhouse.com.

The Ultimatum of GOD NATURE first published in Japanese in 1996. This selection
has been taken from the English-language edition, Sowing Seeds in the Desert
(Chelsea Green Publishing, 2012), translated and edited by Larry Korn.
This selection published in Penguin Books 2021

001

Copyright © The Masanobu Fukuoka Estate, 2012

Set in 11.5/14pt Dante MT Std
Typeset by Jouve (UK), Milton Keynes
Printed and bound in Great Britain by Clays Ltd, Elcograf S.p.A.

The authorized representative in the EEA is Penguin Random House Ireland,
Morrison Chambers, 32 Nassau Street, Dublin D02 YH68

A CIP catalogue record for this book is available from the British Library

ISBN: 978-0-241-51444-3

www.greenpenguin.co.uk

Contents

The Call to Natural Farming

Fifty years ago, I had an experience that changed my life forever. I was twenty-five years old at the time. After graduating from Gifu Agricultural College in plant pathology, I took a job with the Plant Inspection Division of the government's Customs Bureau inspecting plants that were coming into or leaving the country. A believer in science, I spent most of my time peering into a microscope in the laboratory, which was located beside a small park in the Yamate area of Yokohama.

After about three years there, without warning, I was stricken with acute pneumonia, which brought me face-to-face with the fear of death. After I recovered, I began questioning the meaning of human existence. Immersed in my distress, I wandered through the hills, day and night.

After one full night of aimlessly wandering, I collapsed, exhausted, at the foot of a tree on a bluff overlooking the harbor. I sat in a daze, drifting in and out of sleep as dawn approached. Suddenly the piercing cry of a night heron awakened me as if from a dream. All the confusion, all the agony that had obsessed me disappeared with the morning mist. Something I call 'true nature' was revealed. I had been transformed, body and soul. The first words that rose to my lips were, 'There is really nothing at all.' I looked around in joyful amazement.

The peaceful beauty of the world became vividly apparent to me. I was overcome with emotion and reduced to trembling. I had been foolishly searching for something when it had been there, right in front of me, all this time.

The sparkle of the morning dew, the green of the trees bathed in morning sunlight, the delightful chatter of birds gathered in the dawn . . . what a wonder it was that I, too, was able to take my place in this realm of freedom, this world of ecstasy.

I saw nature directly. It was pure and radiant, what I imagined heaven to be.

I saw the mountains and rivers, the grasses and trees, the flowers, the small birds and the butterflies as if for the first time. I felt the throbbing of life, delighted in hearing the songbirds and the sound of rustling leaves. I became as light as the wings of a dragonfly, and felt as if I were flying as high as the mountain peaks.

The question is why, on that occasion alone, did the world that I was used to seeing every day appear so fresh and new and move me so deeply? To be honest, my mind at the time was not in its usual state. I had reached the point of mental and spiritual exhaustion from my sickness and had no strength of will left. In the soft, tranquil air of daybreak, I was neither waiting for the dawn nor looking about for anything in particular. All of a sudden, with that heron's single cry, I was awakened. My heart opened and I was unable to stop my ceaseless flow of tears.

In a single leaf, a single flower, I was moved to appreciate all the beautiful forms of this world. What I saw was simply the green of the trees sparkling in sunlight. I saw no deity other than the trees themselves, nor did I perceive a spirit or soul of vegetation hidden within the trees. When I viewed the world with an empty mind, I was able to perceive that the world before me was the true form of nature, and the only deity I would ever worship.

The experience I had that morning is indelibly impressed in my mind, its freshness undimmed even today. But realistically, I could not expect those feelings to last forever.

I was brimming with self-confidence, convinced that I had come to possess the wisdom of truth. I felt that I could solve all the problems of the world. But as the days passed, the whirlwind of emotion abated, and the true form of nature, which had been so clear to me, gradually receded. While my viewpoint might have changed, it did not necessarily mean that I myself had undergone a fundamental change.

It took a few years to be able to integrate this new understanding into my daily life, but the first thing I did was to quit my job with the Customs Bureau. I set out from the Boso Peninsula in Chiba Prefecture and wandered westward for a month or two, stopping here and there along the way. I danced in the beauty of nature as I traveled, reaching Kyushu as winter approached.

During my travels I talked with a number of people about my realization. In those discussions I could see that my ideas were at odds with the way the rest of society was thinking at the time. When I said that humankind lives in an unreal world separate from nature, I was told that I was simply deluding myself. Eventually, since I could find no words to adequately express what I had seen that morning, I learned that it was better to remain silent. As time went on, that pure vision of nature I had experienced grew weaker and weaker.

Had I been the sort of person to immerse myself in religious discipline, I suppose I would have renewed my vows. But being at heart a carefree individual, I chose to pursue a life of farming, separating myself from the commotion of modern society.

My Return to Farming

After spending some time living in a lakeshore hut outside the town of Beppu, I returned to my parents' farm in Ehime Prefecture on Shikoku Island. It was the spring of 1938. I began living alone in a hut in the citrus orchard, and decided to start a natural farm to express what I had seen that morning in physical form. Most importantly, I wanted to demonstrate how my ideas could be of practical benefit to society.

At first, I was not sure how to go about it, but I was resolved to making the orchard at the top of the hill into a paradise. My idea was to let nature have a free hand. At the time, the citrus trees my father planted had been carefully shaped, but because I failed to prune them – with the idea that they would revert to their natural form – the branches grew out every which way, insects and diseases appeared, and before I knew it I had wiped out more than two hundred trees.

This first experiment, simply doing nothing, was a magnificent failure. It was not natural farming; it was abandonment. But I was pleased that at least I had learned from that disaster the difference between non-intervention and taking human responsibility.

My father was worried about me, but I persisted. Unfortunately, however, the tide of human history carried me in an unexpected and unwanted direction. The skies over Asia had become dark and dangerous. Soldiers were marching off to war, and the drumbeat grew louder and louder. My surroundings lost their serenity. It was no longer possible to turn my back on the world and live alone and carefree in my hillside hut.

My father, who was mayor of the village at the time, urged me to find work somewhere, anywhere, even at an agricultural experiment station. It was a time when the government and the farmers were pouring all their efforts into increasing food production, so I decided, after an absence of five years, to return to work for the government as a plant pathologist. I obeyed my father's wishes and left the farm.

Here is something I scribbled in my hut at that time.

> *Wishing to cultivate the earth,*
> *I cultivate understanding.*
> *In vain I wield my hoe*
> *And sharpen my sickle.*
> *The earth languishes, grasses and trees wither,*
> *Gazing at heaven and earth and heaving a long sigh,*
> *I am filled with despair.*

When will
That Garden of Eden
Bloom again?

That small hermitage, Musoan, commemorates the birthplace of natural farming, but there is no trace of it left today. That simple mud-walled hut has, over time, simply returned to the earth.

Challenges During Wartime

And so I spent the years of World War II at the agricultural experiment station in Kochi Prefecture on Shikoku. Looking back, I was completely irresponsible while working there. Instead of concentrating on my research about blight and insect damage in plants, I argued with my co-workers, asking them to consider my ideas denying the validity of science. Or else, under the pretense of investigating plant diseases and insect pests, I rambled through the mountainous interior of Kochi doing my own research about nature. I had one foot in natural farming and the other in the world of science. My life was full of contradictions.

As Japan's policies were leading the country into war, I deeply regretted that I could do nothing to stop it. One Sunday, five or six young soldiers from the nearby air force unit came to visit on their day off. I welcomed them, of course. I wanted to offer them something, but there was no food. So they just spent the entire day relaxing in my upstairs room and then went back to the base. The following morning they disappeared into the southern sky. It still breaks my heart to recall the boyish faces of those young men.

As Japan entered the last year of the war, I, too, was drafted. Luckily the war ended soon after and I was spared. I received my discharge and gratefully returned home. I was finally back working in the fields again, savoring the joy of simply being alive. I especially remember the buoyant sound of the threshing machine as I treaded it for the first time after a long absence.

Since that time, I have been a farmer, never veering from the path of natural farming. I experienced many failures as I developed my natural method for growing rice and winter grains in an unplowed field, broadcasting the seeds right onto the surface of the soil, but I persisted. I was also interested in creating a natural orchard without cultivating the land, using chemicals, or doing hand weeding. Before I knew it, forty years had passed. This is not to say that I was a particularly industrious farmer. Actually, I was aiming at a do-nothing method of farming.

Yes, many years have passed since the inspiration of my youth. I am a white-haired old man now. When I look back on the postwar period, it seems so long ago and yet it seems so short. As I consider the few years that remain to me, I wonder if I have done all that I could have.

The road I have taken has been a single path. The starting point of this journey, it turns out, is also its end.

The True Meaning of Nature

I spent many years of my youth foolishly searching for something I 'should' have been doing. Instead, I should have entrusted everything to the flowers blooming in the meadow. Even if people do nothing at all, the grasses and trees and the songbirds will live on.

The poet Basho composed the haiku, 'Ah, how sacred / the light of the sun / on young green leaves.' Indeed – I can clasp my hands in reverence and kneel before the daikon flower. Even if I cannot make a poem as beautiful as Basho's, my heart is singing, 'Oh, the whiteness of the daikon flower / the radiance, the splendor!'

The sad truth is that for much of my youth, I, too, felt estranged from nature. But now I just take a single flower in my hand and converse with it. I have finally learned that, although nature does not reach out to people directly, people can always approach nature and seek salvation that way.

In ancient times, I would like to think that people must have made drawing close to nature the most important goal in their lives.

Once long ago, when I was in the mountains, I unconsciously wrote, 'The mountains, rivers, grasses and trees are all Buddha,' on a piece of wood. At other times I would suggest that 'God' refers to the absolute truth that transcends time and space. Perhaps an even better description, I sometimes thought, was Lao-tse's term 'The Nameless.' I was really just struggling with words. Actually, I think people would be better off without words altogether.

The Errors of Human Thought

Because of the rapid development of modern science, the Asian tendency to live quietly and view the world as transitory is disappearing. The new trend is toward glorifying modern civilization and the idea that the material is almighty.

Within the history of the development of Western science, the epoch-making discoveries that have had the greatest influence on the human race are (1) the theory of biological evolution advanced in

Darwin's *The Origin of Species,* (2) Newton's universal gravitation and Galileo's heliocentric theory, and (3) Einstein's relativity theory of the universe.

Darwin started with the progress of human beings on earth and followed the traces of the origin and development of living things, eventually determining that living things have evolved. The idea that human beings must continue to develop became firmly rooted in people's minds.

Newton, seeing how an apple fell, discovered the law of universal gravitation and laid the foundation for modern physics. Galileo understood that the earth was round and, when placed on trial by the church, did not falter in expounding his theory that the earth revolves around the sun. By denying the fallacy that the heavens revolve around the earth, he dealt a serious blow to the theory of divine creation.

By establishing the relativity theory of the universe, Einstein propelled the human race into the space age. To everyone's amazement, he concluded that there is no speed faster than the speed of light, overturned the commonly accepted belief that light always travels the shortest distance in a straight line, and proposed the new theory that light is curved.

In addition, Einstein said that light waves, radio waves, and electromagnetic waves are all the same and that they travel through space at a fixed speed, regardless of their length, without accelerating. From his formula that mass and energy are equivalent, the launch of man-made satellites and space vehicles became possible.

The religion of Buddhism, however, rejects knowledge acquired through the human intellect as nothing more than illusion. Some Western myths are also skeptical of human knowledge, teaching that since Adam and Eve ate the fruit of the Tree of Knowledge, humankind has been banished from the Garden of Eden.

Western philosophy has been divided on this issue, however. Socrates, for one, started with the assumption that human beings know nothing. Descartes, on the other hand, declared, 'I think, therefore I am.' Beginning with that conviction, that people can and do know themselves, he made human judgment his standard, established rules for the physical world, and began analyzing its properties.

Scientists have historically assumed that it is acceptable to control nature using human will. Nature is seen as the 'outside world' in opposition to humanity, and this idea forms the basis of modern scientific civilization. But this fictitious 'I' of Descartes can never fully comprehend the true state of reality.

Just as human beings do not know themselves, they cannot know the other. Human beings may be the children of 'Mother Nature,' but they are no longer able to see the true form of their mother. Looking for the whole, they only see the parts. Seeing their mother's breast, they mistake it for the mother herself. If someone does not know his mother, he is a child who does not know whose child he is. He is like a monkey, raised in a zoo by humans, who is convinced that the zookeeper is his mother.

Similarly, the discriminating and analytical knowledge of scientists may be useful for taking nature apart and looking at its parts, but it is of no use for grasping the reality of pure nature. One day scientists will realize how limiting and misguided it is to hack nature to pieces like that.

I sometimes make a brush-and-ink drawing to illustrate this point. I call it 'the cave of the intellect.' It shows two men toiling in a pit or a cave swinging their pickaxes to loosen the hard earth. The picks represent the human intellect. The more these workers swing their tools, the deeper the pit gets and the more difficult it is for them to escape. Outside the cave, I draw a person who is relaxing in the sunlight. While still working to provide everyday necessities through natural farming, that person is free from the drudgery of trying to understand nature, and is simply enjoying life.

Ironically, nature is also being damaged by people who pride themselves on following a path of moderation, who may think they have nature's best interest at heart.

These well-meaning people, known for their compassion and practical sense, might say:

'Human beings have lived in nature for thousands and thousands of years, sometimes joyfully, sometimes filled with sorrow. Isn't that the essence of the relationship between people and nature? Isn't it simplistic to see nature as only filled with truth, good, and beauty while seeing human beings as insensitive and ignorant?' At first glance, this opinion seems sensible, and appears to be an objective point of view. But these goodhearted people have not escaped the realm of relative thinking.

Seen from a nonrelative perspective, nature transcends beauty and ugliness, good and evil. Whether we see this world as filled with contradictions, or as existing in perfect harmony, is determined by whether we analyze it using our intellect, or grasp the entirety of nature without making any distinctions at all. It is only by doing the latter that we can see nature's true form.

No God or Buddha Will Rescue the Human Race

The destruction of nature will lead to the destruction of the human race, but many people seem to be convinced that even if humans should disappear, they will be brought to life again by the hand of their god. This idea, however, is nothing more than fantasy. The human race will not be born again. When the people on the earth have died out, there will be no God or Buddha to rescue them.

People do sometimes sense the sacredness of nature, such as when they look closely at a flower, climb high peaks, or journey deep into the mountain. Such aesthetic sense, love, receptivity, and under-standing are people's most basic instincts – their true nature. These days, however, humans are flying in a completely different direction to some unknown des-tination, and they seem to be doing it as rapidly as possible.

Perhaps the people who most easily perceive that nature is sacred are a few religious people, artists of great sensitivity, and children. With their compassion they often perceive, at the very least, that nature is something beyond human invention and that it should be revered. The poets who write about nature, the painters who turn it into works of art, the people who compose music, the sculptors . . . I would like to believe that they are the ones drawn to what is truly meaningful.

But if an artist's understanding of nature is unclear, no matter how keen his sensitivity, no matter how excellent his power of expression, no matter how refined his technique, he will eventually find himself lost.

The Dragonfly Will Be the Messiah

There has never been a generation like the present where people's hearts are so badly wounded. This is true of every area of society – politics, economics, education, and culture. It is reflected in the degradation of the environment, which comes about through the material path humanity has chosen. Now we have the ugly sight of industry, government, and the military joining forces in the struggle for ultimate power.

In the present age of disintegration the various religions of the world, old and new, large and small, are becoming very active. Indeed, whenever the world has fallen into disorder, religious movements have flourished.

Let me give one example of a religion that promises wealth and good fortune. A young man who was worshiped as the founder of a new religion in Kobe came to my farm with ten or so of his disciples. This fellow told me that he had received special training to transform him from an ordinary religious person to the founder of this new religion. He learned such things as physiognomy, mind reading, fortune-telling, palmistry, divination, hypnotism for healing disease, exorcism, and various ways of communicating divine messages, such as writing in sand. He told me in great detail about the schemes he had used to get believers into the palm of his hand, starting with tricks for determining a potential believer's character flaws and problems. This, he said, would help him attract new followers.

This is only one type of many religious imposters who hold both the deities and the people captive and run around acquiring believers in order to make money and gain power. But many of them are popular and well regarded, and would not seem to be the stereotypical image of an imposter. This paradox leads me to reflect on how human beings are nothing more than animals dancing to a tune piped by their own ideas.

I look forward to the day when there is no need for sacred scriptures or sutras. The dragonfly will be the messiah.

A Life of Natural Culture

When I mention that human society is on the wrong path, I often hear the retort, 'Then show me a better one.' Because it does not have a name yet, I will refer to it as 'natural culture and community.' Natural culture is simply a way of life in which people enjoy the truth and beauty of nature, a life in which people, with freedom in their hearts, climb mountains, play in meadows, bathe in the warm rays of sunlight, breathe pure air, drink crystalline water, and experience the true joy of life. The society I am describing is one in which people will create a free and generous community.

Once the primal source of nature is destroyed, however, it will no longer be able to restore itself, and this image of a natural culture will become obsolete. Indeed, many species of plants and animals become extinct each day, and the meaning of the disappearance of one bird or one plant is not just the death of that bird or that plant. It is of grave significance to us all. It is connected with the destruction of the harmony of all living things.

If humanity can regain its original kinship with nature, we should be able to live in peace and abundance. Seen through the eyes of modern civilization, however, this life of natural culture must appear to be monotonous and primitive, but not to me.

There are many other people besides me who question the path of modern society. They are filled with foreboding, wondering whether or not we can solve, or somehow evade, the current environmental crisis.

There are even many scientists who believe that the long-term sustainability of life on earth, from the standpoint of the natural environment and its resources, will be decided in the next twenty or thirty years. It is these people to whom I speak directly.

We must realize that both in the past and today, there is only one 'sustainable' course available to us. We must find our way back to true nature. We must set ourselves to the task of revitalizing the earth. Regreening the earth, sowing seeds in the desert – that is the path society must follow. My travels around the world have convinced me of that.

Reconsidering Human Knowledge

The human race first appeared on earth a couple of million years ago, and we began living what people generally consider 'civilized' life several thousand years ago. In Japan, however, people began living a 'civilized' life only in the last few hundred years. With the rapid development of science and technology, without our even having time to figure out where we are going, it seems that modern civilization has peaked and that disorder is emerging on a worldwide scale. But is the conclusion to this unfortunate chapter in human history inevitable? What will happen to the world in the future?

The Birth of Discriminating Knowledge

From the time that a child sees the moon floating in the sky and says, 'I see the moon,' human knowing begins. When a child first becomes aware of the moon, that child is simply filled with wonder. Then after a period of time the child learns to discriminate between a subject, 'I,' and an object, 'the moon.' The child comes to know the thing called the moon as 'other.' So even in the structure of human language, human beings are taught to set themselves apart from nature. The intimate and harmonious relationship between people and nature that once existed – which we can see in children's instinctive wonderment – becomes cold and distant.

Even if we say that we know the green of nature, this is merely the understanding that discriminates green from other colors. If we have not grasped the *intrinsic* greenness of the grasses and trees, which originates with the life at their core, we cannot say that we really understand what true green is. People simply believe they understand by making a distinction based on the outer appearance.

If knowledge of a whole (one) is broken into two and explained, and then these are divided into three and four and analyzed, we are no closer to understanding the whole than we were before. When we do this, however, we come under the illusion that knowledge has increased. But can we say that by endlessly repeating our divisions and analyses and then gathering up all the fragments, we have advanced human knowledge in any meaningful way?

No matter how much we accumulate, synthesize, and make judgments, this effort is not useful for clarifying the true state of things. Furthermore, it throws us into confusion. Once people create a mental image of the 'moon,' the moon takes concrete form and we want to 'know the moon,' and then discover more and more about the moon. This desire eventually leads to actually traveling to the moon and retrieving stones to bring back to earth for further research. The next thing you know we are building space stations, and who knows what else might follow.

With increased 'knowledge' comes an increased desire for *more* knowledge, and then people work and work to invent machines to help them achieve even greater knowledge. But even if 'proof' is found, only more questions will arise from that so-called proof. The desire for knowledge becomes endless and we lose sight of our place in the world. In the end, the true essence of the moon is more clearly seen through the eyes of a child.

Darwin's Theory of Natural Selection

Darwin's theory of natural selection gives a good illustration of the principle that although the discriminating knowledge of science may seem useful for taking nature apart and analyzing the fragments, it is of no use for grasping the reality of nature.

The Darwinian theory of evolution breaks down the 4.6 billion years since the earth came into being, observes the living things that came into existence at certain times and places, and examines their mutual relationships. Based on this, the diversification and systematic development of the organisms are inferred and classified, and this is all developed into his theory of evolution.

In other words, when oxygen and water formed on the planet – which, in the beginning, was apparently an inorganic mass – primitive life-forms began to appear. These evolved and new life-forms appeared. At first, extremely simple microorganisms such as fungi and bacteria were born; then they developed and branched out, organisms of other forms were born, and gradually the more complicated higher plants and animals began to multiply upon the earth.

The idea is that the life-forms on earth came into being in sequence, along with the development of the earth itself. Various life-forms appeared and lived as part of the food web, but only those that successfully adapted to their environment survived. This is known as the theory of natural selection, the theory of the most adaptable, and sometimes popularly referred to as the survival of the fittest. Among all the life-forms, those that are selected by nature and survive the struggle for existence obtain the right to live and reproduce.

One question I have about this theory is: What basis was used to determine which species are higher or lower, and which are strong or weak? To decide that the phenomenon of the survival of the fittest is the providence of nature and that people are the highest, most evolved species seems to reflect more the strongman logic of human beings than the true state of nature. Actually, no one can say which species is the strongest because all living things depend on one another to survive, reproduce, and eventually decompose, so life can go on for all.

It is true that all forms of life – by necessity and by natural design – consume one another to live, but they do not intentionally bring about another's extinction, systematically deprive other species of their source of food, or create factions and wars. The same cannot be said for human beings.

In nature's cyclical rhythms, there are no grounds for the discriminatory view that underlies Darwin's view of superiority and inferiority that deems single-celled organisms as lower, and more complicated life forms as higher. It would be more appropriate to say we are all one continuous life-form.

Whether you see differences between butterflies

and moths, dragonflies and fireflies, depends on whether you are looking at the big picture or the small one. In the eyes of children, frogs, fish, birds, and squirrels all appear to be the same friends, but the eyes of adults are drawn to the differences in appearance and form, and so they appear to be different animals.

Viewing the world macroscopically or microscopically simply means that different scales are being used. Depending on whether you use human time, measured in minutes and seconds, or the eternal time of the Ganges River – or whether your field of vision is as narrow as the inside of a box or as wide as the universe – the appearance of the world changes completely.

Similarly, there is a common belief that there is a great difference between living and nonliving things, but even that distinction occurs only because of one's perception.

Understanding True Time and Space

The commonsense understanding of time is that it is a direct, linear flow from the past through the present to the future. Darwin's theory of evolution is based on this idea of human, historical time. The organisms are classified into fragments in time and location, and systematized. This systemization emphasizes the differences among them. Species that were originally brothers and sisters became divided in people's thinking, by being made into distinctly different things.

Transcendent time, or time as it exists in nature, is a continuous moment of the present. When one sees and operates within that time and space, it is the *unity* of all things that is perceived.

The idea of time that people generally accept came into being with the invention of the calendar and the clock. But a clock, with its needle going around a series of numbers, is just a means of counting.

Time does not simply flow mechanically in a straight line in a fixed direction. We could think of time as flowing up and down, right and left, forward and backward. As time develops and expands, multifaceted and three-dimensional, the past is concealed within the instant of the present, and within this instant of time is concealed the eternity of the future.

It is easy to liken the flow of time to the flow of a river. But even the phenomenon of water flowing in a river presents challenges of perception. When you stand on a riverbank and look at the water, you can clearly see that the water is flowing in one direction. But if you are in a boat moving at the same speed as the water, the river does not seem to be flowing at all; rather the riverbank appears to be moving upstream.

As a Zen master once said. 'The river does not flow. The bridge flows.'

The Rising and Sinking of Genes

Many years ago, when I was a young man working as a microbiologist, bacteriophages – viruses that infect and consume bacteria – were discovered. They were said to be the first-known nonliving things that reproduced. I was quite interested in them as some intermediate matter between living and nonliving things. (By now, of course, research on viruses has further blurred the boundary between living and nonliving things.) When looked at from the standpoint of their elemental particles, the distinction between animate and inanimate, living and nonliving things, plants, animals, viruses, gases, and minerals becomes inconsequential.

The fact that the structure of DNA, and the genetic code by which this genetic material is translated into protein, is the same for all living things indicates to me that all living things are fundamentally related. These proteins could be seen as the liaison between living and nonliving forms and so play the role of threads tying the living and nonliving together.

So, while there seems to be a great difference

between plants and human beings, their genetic material is the same. Whether something becomes a plant or a human being is just a question of whether or not the genetic factor for greenery surfaces or sinks. In fact, only a small portion of the combinations of the four genetic elements have successfully come into being, while most of the other combinations have been lost or are dormant.

The reason that there are so few intermediary forms between species and that we cannot find fossils of them is not necessarily because they did not exist. Rather than saying that the genes that become intermediate species have not functioned at all, we can only assume that even if they *were* born, they died in infancy and did not come to the attention of human beings. That is why different, seemingly disconnected species and varieties are left.

It is like an acacia tree that produces millions of seeds, each with its own distinctive genetic makeup. Few of them actually germinate and thrive. After ten years, perhaps only one or two trees will survive as the descendants of the parent tree, but all the other trees that did not survive were also possible.

Take the islands of Japan's Seto Inland Sea for another example. The many islands in this sea have various shapes, they have been given different names, and they appear to be separate islands, but they are all connected at the bottom of the sea, so you could consider them all the same single 'island of Japan.' On a larger scale, of course, one could say that they are connected to all the islands and continents of the world by being part of the earth's crust. In the same way, the animals and plants living on earth appear to be different, but they also are all connected at the base. Whether the genes survive, surfacing like islands floating in the Inland Sea, or do not, sinking beneath the water, depends on the arrangement of the genes and on the constant rearrangement of subatomic particles.

An Alternative View of Evolution

Perhaps it went like this: The Creator rolled the seeds of every living thing into clay pellets and gave them to messengers to scatter randomly. Some seeds were programmed to become active soon after the birth of the earth. Others were programmed to thrive in water. Some were suited to the mountains, some to the deserts. The seeds that were designed to become human beings were made to come to life during the later ages of the earth.

Millions of seeds were broadcast at one time, and the living things of the world took on various forms.

Some became microorganisms, some became green plants, and some became animals that could run around.

Scientifically, we could say that these seeds germinated when conditions were right for their germination, and only those that took forms suited to their living environment developed and survived. Those seeds that fell into the sea became seaweed, coral, and sea anemones, others became shellfish and shrimp, and all lived together.

The seeds scattered in marshes became cattails, some changed into catfish or eels, and in some cases the same seeds became frogs, turtles, or snakes. Living things bearing similar genes but manifesting differently became forest trees, while others became the birds that lived in the forest trees. At the same time that the vegetation on earth increased and large trees grew in abundance, large animals such as tigers and elephants made their appearance. Microorganisms, plants, and animals are all genetic siblings, of course, but each appeared in a different costume.

In some ways, this may seem like a distorted dramatization of Darwin's theory of evolution. The big difference is how we think about the passage of time. In my mind, millions and millions of years appear as a momentary flash. Consequently, the innumerable varieties of living things have not originated at different times in different places, but rather at the same time, and in the same place.

Nature is one body. We can say that while human beings and insects are part of nature, they also represent nature as a whole. And if that is so, when we harm plants, microorganisms, and insects through large-scale conventional agriculture (to use just one example), we are harming humanity as well.

I would like to propose a dharma wheel theory of biological development as an alternative to Darwin's flat, single-plane theory of natural selection. I will call it the Dharma Wheel Theory of Flux in All Things. The dharma wheel can be seen as a representation of natural law. Nature expands in all directions, three-dimensionally, and at the same time, as it develops, it converges and contracts. We can see these changes of expansion and contraction as a kind of wheel. It is like the universe – three-dimensional, always expanding and contracting, spinning in space, and heading in an unknown direction.

At the creation, along with the birth of the rest of the universe, the earth and all the living things on it were born as a single, unified body with a common fate. Everything regarding the roles, the aims, and the work of each of them originated and was concluded in the same instant. All things were designed so that one is many, the individual is the whole, the whole is perfect, there is no waste, nothing is useless, and all things perform their best service.

There is another aspect to this dynamic, spinning, expanding, and contracting three-dimensional and multifaceted dharma wheel. Its center, the hub, is forever motionless and forever one. Instead of seeing the distinctions among the things of this world, if we look at the base, it is all one, and the purpose of all things is the same.

Naturally Occurring Hybrids in My Rice Fields

Ten or so years ago, I tried crossbreeding nonglutinous rice from Burma with Japanese glutinous rice in order to develop a new variety suited to natural farming. The two rices are extremely different in character, but the genetic characteristics of the parents were intermingled, so I wound up getting twenty, thirty, sometimes several hundred different varieties. When I arranged these varieties, I noticed that their characteristics formed a continuum.

There was nonglutinous rice close to glutinous, intermediate forms, glutinous rice close to nonglutinous, and some in which glutinous and nonglutinous, and some in which glutinous and nonglutinous grains were mixed together on a single head. Some rice plants reached a height of only ten or twelve inches, while others were giants more than five feet tall. There was also a succession of different colors of rice – white, red, and blackish brown. Some were flavorful, some not, some powdery, some sticky. In this situation, it was impossible to say which was good and which was bad. I also came to question the value of distinguishing between glutinous and nonglutinous rices, and even between paddy and dry field culture.

After years of crossbreeding rice in my fields, however, I finally concluded that on a natural farm, people do not need to create new varieties by artificial crossbreeding at all, since the insects that most people consider as harmful were creating new varieties on their own.

In my rice fields, I noticed that after locusts and other insects had chewed round holes in the rice grains just as the heads were sprouting, slugs, snails, cutworms, and other creatures came along and crawled over the grains at night. They ate down to the stamens in the holes, after which windblown pollen from other varieties adhered and achieved fertilization. In other words, rice, which is said to be self-pollinating, can also be pollinated by other plants, and in this way new varieties arise naturally.

In a conventionally farmed paddy field sprayed with insecticide, natural hybrids do not occur. On a natural farm, however, they can easily survive, and there are many chances for new varieties to appear. In the end, there is no need for people to imitate nature by carrying out artificial crossbreeding. It is all being done for them.

Alongside crossbreeding rice with rice, I experimented with crossbreeding rice with weeds such as deccan grass (*Echinochloa colona*) and foxtail (wild rye) and was thinking that if that went well, I would try more combinations with foxtail millet and Chinese millet, but my original purpose was not to study rice for its own sake. I was really just amusing myself by going in the opposite direction of what was being recommended by agronomists at the time. I was doing a reverse breeding in search of atavisms: potentially valuable species that had been lost over the centuries.

With today's technology, I undoubtedly would have succeeded should I have taken my research any farther, but I did not have the slightest intention of setting foot in the domain of the biological sciences. I stopped at the point of confirming the possibility. When I saw insects were creating a succession of new varieties in the fields of my natural farm, I thought it would be better to leave things up to them, and I stepped back.

I also came to the conclusion that the classification of plants, placing them in species, genus, family, and order, was not only an imposition on the plants, but of no use at all to human beings. We would be better off simply appreciating all the diverse forms nature has provided and not interfering.

With the current technology of gene exchange, it has become easy to create different varieties of fruits and vegetables. I call it 'the mad course of genetic engineering.' Soon humans will acquire the technology to turn animals into plants, and plants into animals. But not only is such scientific meddling unnecessary, it is dangerous. If we follow Darwin's thinking, that one form of life evolved into the millions of life-forms that exist today, then it seems justifiable to add a few new species or genera here and there. People may hope that they can create even better organisms and that these new forms will assimilate with nature's creatures, but the result will be the opposite.

By creating new organisms through biological engineering, people take the risk of throwing the natural plot of the world play into confusion. Even if we understand that the functioning of the genes of living things is determined by the way the four bases of DNA are arranged, it is optimistic to suppose that genetically engineered plants and animals will not get out of control.

There is so much in this world that we do not understand, not only about the shapes and forms of living things, but also about their temperaments and spirit. When we try something like creating new life-forms and then turn them loose in the environment, disastrous side effects are *certain* to occur – we just do not know exactly what these side effects will be yet.

Abandoning What We Think We Know

Ten years ago I paid a visit to the niece of Albert Einstein, near Central Park in New York City. When I asked her if Einstein thought that time and space really existed, she replied that although he saw time and space as relative, he probably could not give an opinion about their reality. That might well have been his answer, if I had been talking to Einstein himself, but we will never really know.

What we *do* know is that he said that mass and matter are energy. We know that extensions of this idea led to enormous energy explosions by splitting the atom. Nuclear physicists realized that if atoms could be split, they could also be fused, and so, brushing aside Einstein's second thoughts, they created the hydrogen bomb. Einstein must still be drifting around in purgatory, burdened with responsibility for his part in this tragedy. I cannot speak for him, of course, but

I imagine he would enjoy a conversation about the limitations of human knowledge.

Some years ago, Fritjof Capra, a professor of theoretical physics at the University of California who also lectures on science as a holistic discipline, visited my hillside hut. He was troubled that the current theories of subatomic particles appeared to be incomplete. There ought to be some fundamental principle, Capra said, and he wanted to express it mathematically.

In searching for this elusive fundamental principle, he had found a hint in the Taoist concept of yin and yang. He called it the science of the Tao, but he added that this alone did not solve the puzzle.

He had likened the lively dance of subatomic particles to the dance of the Indian god Shiva, but it was difficult to know what the steps of the dance were, or the melody of the flute. I had learned about the concept of subatomic particles from him, so of course I had no words that could directly dispel his frustration.

It is one thing to think that within the constant changes of all things and phenomena there must be some corresponding fixed laws, but humans cannot seem to be satisfied until they have expressed these laws mathematically. I believe there is a limit to our ability to know nature with human knowledge. When I mentioned this might be the source of his problem, Capra countered, saying, 'I've written more than ten books, but haven't you written books, too, thinking knowledge was useful?'

'It's true that I have written several books,' I responded, 'but you seem to have written your books believing they would be useful to other people. I've written mine with the idea that books are not useful at all. It appears that both of us, from the West and the East, are investigating nature and yearning for a return to nature, so we are able to sit together and have a meeting of the minds. But on the point of affirming or negating human knowledge, we seem to be moving in opposite directions, so we probably will not arrive at the same place in the end.'

In the end, it will require some courage and perhaps a leap of faith for people to abandon what they think they know.

Healing a World In Crisis

I read about a professor recently who did a basic study of the deserts of Iran and Iraq. I do not remember his name anymore, but he came to the conclusion that it would be better to leave the deserts as they are, and refrain from intervening. There is also a theory that it would be better to let Africa's deserts and the resulting public health problems take their 'natural' course.

When considering these issues, we should begin by asking ourselves what is normal and what is abnormal. If a desert is naturally occurring, then it is better not to interfere, but if it exists as an abnormal condition, then we have no choice but to help restore it to health. It is clear that in many desert areas nature has been laid to waste and food has become scarce as a result of human activity. Now we must pay the price and take responsibility by repairing the damage.

If we investigate scientifically what is right or wrong, healthy or ill about the earth, and also the health and illness of human beings, we may seem to understand, but there are no absolute standards for making such judgments. Better to consider all things from the beginning with an open mind.

Restoring the Earth and Its People

With our current system of observation and judgment, human beings cannot decide whether the deserts are a kind of cancer making the earth sick, or a phenomenon of self-cleaning – a change by which the earth achieves balance. People see the population increase in Africa, China, and India as tragic, but who is it that has brought about the disappearance of vegetation and the scarcity of food there?

In the past, present, and future, the true disposition of nature is toward abundance for human beings and for all species. Therefore, the question should not be 'Why are there too many people?' but rather, 'Who has created the scarcity into which they are born?' And then, finally, 'How can we heal the earth so it can support future generations?' It is too simplistic to begin and end the conversation with a limited view of overpopulation. Better to ask: Why must people suffer so? And have we done all we can to alleviate the pain of the earth and the pain of the human race?

It is important to reflect on what has happened historically in regard to agriculture and medicine. We have seen huge advances in modern medicine, but there is little value in the advancement of medicine if the number of sick people continues to increase. It is the same with modern agriculture. How can we congratulate ourselves on the advances in modern agriculture, including greatly increased production, if the rate of starvation, scarcity, depletion, and disease increases even more rapidly?

In Nature, There Are No Beneficial or Harmful Insects

During the years I have watched the development of my natural farm, I have seen little damage done to fruits, vegetables, or grains. The crops have grown vigorously and lived natural lives without withering and dying prematurely. That does not mean it is pest- or insect-free. If you looked closely, you would observe many insects on the fruit trees and many diseased leaves. The damage they cause makes up no more than 5 percent, but that amount must be allocated to provide food for birds and insects and to thin out the weakest individuals.

Plants, people, butterflies, and dragonflies appear

to be separate, individual living things, yet each is an equal and important participant in nature. They share the same mind and life spirit. They form a single living organism. To speak of creatures as beneficial insects, harmful insects, pathogenic bacteria, or troublesome birds is like saying the right hand is good and the left hand is bad. Nature is an endless cycle, in which all things participate in the same dance of life and death, living together and dying together.

Eastern and Western Medicine

In Western medicine, the body is first examined to determine which parts are ailing, and then an attempt is made to heal the ailment. That is, doctors use a localized, external treatment of symptoms. If you have a pain in your head, doctors will order a CT scan, analyze the results, surgically remove the 'abnormal' portion, and try to repair the area as best as possible.

In Eastern medicine, doctors start by looking at the eyes and skin coloring, listening to what the person says, and checking the patient's complete mental and physical health. The main objective is to find what constitutes the overall *health* of the individual.

It is thought that in the end, both methods will be

effective in healing, but in fact, they move in opposite directions. They can also be viewed as two poles, one with the goal of healing sickness and the other with the goal of maintaining health.

When the specialized Western medicinal approach is used, the question of what gives life and health to the whole body and mind is put off. In other words, modern Western medicine puts the human body ahead of the human spirit. This separation is a starting point for emotional anxiety among people today.

Eastern medicine, on the other hand, sees a person's natural form and the degree of health of the mind and body, and asks how to *preserve* that health. What is considered the healthy body and spirit must be based on the natural form. But in contemporary society it is becoming increasingly difficult to maintain that natural form, or even remember what it originally was, since people are increasingly living in their minds and disconnected from their bodies. To find what the natural form is for human beings, it is necessary to consider what the appropriate relationship should be between people and nature and how they should live to embody that relationship.

Recently there has been a big hubbub over the question of brain death. This is a confusing issue that involves the question of the biological life and death of human beings, as well as moral questions. It is made even more complicated by the involvement of religious views of life and death. Physicians, by being overly attached to the importance of maintaining life at all cost, often try to extend biological life even if there is no joy and no hope. They blur the boundary between life and death, departing from the realm of science.

Physicians and nurses must be guides to life. They must not specialize in simply healing sickness and giving advice on pain and medication. This means there will be times when they must give people the comfort of living truthfully and simply oversee parting and death. We could say that is the ultimate, most humane medical treatment.

Regarding questions of life and death, I think people would be better off observing how the cycles of life and death occur in nature. Imagine a meadow full of wildflowers and sweet clover with bees and a few spotted fawns grazing in sunlight. Imagine the cycle of seasons – the rhythms of growth and decay, the endless beauty. We can never understand the wonderful ways of this world, but is it not enough to simply enjoy our time here and be grateful? In the end it is love, really, that sustains our spirit. Life without love, life without joy – like a barren meadow attracting no wildlife – leads to an unpleasant environment, a sickly body, and an unhappy existence.

When I asked a Japanese youth where he found happiness, he said, 'I'm happy if my life is filled with fine food and clothing, a nice place to live, a car, leisure time, and foreign travel.' A young fellow from Nepal responded to the same question in this way: 'From *The One-Straw Revolution* I learned that true joy comes from nature, and that we can find it by giving up our attachments.' One was trying to find joy in the midst of human society, the other in the midst of nature. One was hooked on materialism, while the other was seeking to be healed.

In the desert, you can hear the sound of the wind and the sand. It is a sad, dry sound, a whispering, a kind of mournful music. The sorrowful braying of a donkey I heard in the African savanna still lingers in my ears. Wailing and squealing, it was like the cry of a child on the verge of death. The desert is also yearning to be healed.

I feel that I saw the essence of medical treatment in a hospital, if you could call it that, in a desert camp for thousands of Ethiopian refugees. Palm leaves had been placed atop several spindly poles, providing a little shade, and that was the hospital.

There was a yardstick and a scale. A child was considered ill when his or her height was too tall in proportion to the child's weight, and the patient would be given a cup of milk containing a drop of

45

nutritional supplement. Every morning two or three hundred people gathered, including the children and the relatives attending them, but only about twenty or thirty children were deemed as sick. The goal was to be one of those who received a cup of milk that day. The children who received no milk cried and whimpered. They did not cry because they were sick, but because they had been examined and judged to be healthy.

The caring presence of the nurses at this hospital seemed to give people the courage to live. The eyes of the children jumping and playing about the area were beautiful and shining. These children – living in a remote community with no writing and no money – were innocent and openhearted. During my time there, I planted vegetable seeds in the gravel around the hospital with them. Of course, the children understood quite well how wonderful it would be if the area turned a rich green, and vegetables grew up beneath banana and papaya trees, so they gleefully scattered the seeds far and wide.

Gradually I came to realize that the process of saving the desert of the human heart and revegetating the actual desert is actually the same thing.

The Fear of Death

The fear of death, I think, is not so much a fear of the death of the body as it is a fear of the loss of the attachment to wealth and fame, and to the other worldly desires that are a part of everyday life. The degree of one's fear of death is generally proportional to the depth of one's worldly attachments and passions.

So how can we die peacefully if we do not resolve our attachments? The content of these attachments, of course, is nothing more than illusion. It is the same as when a person, believing he possesses a treasure in gold, silver, and jewels, opens the box to find only worthless bits of glass and rubble.

I have said that material things have no intrinsic value. It simply appears that they have value because people have created the conditions in which they *seem* to be valuable. Change the conditions and the value is lost. Value is born and disappears according to the whims of the times.

There is nothing for people to gain and nothing for them to lose. As long as people lived according to natural law, they could die peacefully at any time like withering grasses.

If a person dies naturally, then not only is that person at ease, but the minds of those around him are at peace, and there will be no regrets in the future. Ultimately, the one that announces the coming of death and delivers the final words is not a priest or a physician, but nature. The only thing for people to decide is how they can best achieve a death that complies with nature's will.

The Question of Spirit

People have concluded that the life and death of other living things in nature is the life and death of the physical body, but with human beings there is also the question of whether life ends with death or continues after it. People so agonize over the many ideas on this subject – whether people's souls continue after death, whether there is another world where spirits go after death, whether people are born again – that they can hardly manage to simply die.

We may think we understand when and where our conscious mind originated, but actually, we do not. So what is the reality of the thing imagined to be a spirit or soul? Even if we say it is the mental activity that occurs in the brain, that does not illuminate its true character.

The way we can elucidate the true nature of the mind is to consider it from the standpoint of *mu*, the awareness people have before they become aware of themselves. It is the original mind before Descartes's 'I think.' The 'I' Descartes referred to is nothing more than the ego. It is not the pure, spotless, transcendental mind.

The ultimate goal of the Western philosophers, who are exploring the world of the individual self, and the religious people of the East, who are seeking the transcendent self, is to elucidate the *original* mind that mysteriously occurs as part of existence itself. It is only through nature that we can see this original mind.

Anyway, none of these ideas – life, death, spirit, the soul – escapes the framework of relative thought. They are nothing more than abstract notions built up of judgments and circular reasoning based on human thinking. People have created a world of ghosts called the hereafter. But no matter how much humans search for freedom from the fear of not knowing, in the end, they should just return to the reality of nature and live their lives in peace.

The Money-Sucking Octopus Economy

The first thing I wondered about when I heard the news of the collapse of the Soviet Union was what would happen to the economies of the capitalist countries in years to come. The fundamental doctrines of capitalism and communism differ, of course, in that capitalism concentrates on production and consumption based on free competition, while communism emphasizes production and distribution on an equal and impartial basis. Contrary to popular belief, however, freedom and equality cannot coexist completely separate from imprisonment and inequality. Even if we speak of the freedom of capitalism, one cannot willfully act with *unlimited* freedom, and not everything can be distributed equally, as communism suggests. Freedom and equality exist in the mutual relationship of warp and weft, inseparable from their shadows and from each other. There is little difference in the content of the two, when it comes down to it.

Even if our goal is to protect forests, revegetate the desert, and revolutionize agriculture, if we do not resolve the fundamental problems of economics and people's way of living, we will not be able to accomplish anything.

I have often said that value does not lie in material goods themselves, but when people create the conditions that make them seem necessary, their value increases. The capitalist system is based on the notion of ever-increasing production and consumption of

material goods, and therefore, in the modern economy, people's value or worth comes to be determined
by their possessions. But if people create conditions
and environments that do *not* make those things necessary, the things, no matter what they are, become
valueless. Cars, for example, are not considered to be
of value by people who are not in a hurry.

Economies that aim at production and consumption
of unnecessary products are themselves meaningless.
People could get along perfectly well without unnecessary goods if they lived a life in which nature provided
everything – assuming, of course, that they had access
to the natural world. But this has become increasingly
difficult in the wake of commodity agriculture and the
global dominance of agribusiness.

Indeed, one can ask of capitalism: 'Why are human
beings not satisfied, as are the birds, with what they
can glean? Why do they earn their sustenance by the
sweat of their brows and suffer so?'

I still remember the words of an Ethiopian tribes-
man who at first rejected my ideas of natural farming.
'Are you asking me to become a farmer?' he asked. 'To
be attached to the soil and to accumulate things are
the acts of a degraded person.' This proud nomad's
words are a perceptive criticism of modern society.

The time seems long ago when the more of something there was, the less expensive it was; when

you could earn a profit simply by producing the things people needed – the age of local small-scale economies.

Even though pumpkins will support the lives of hundreds of people, when it became more profitable to deal in diamonds, which weigh only a few grams each, everyone stopped growing pumpkins. Once the distribution system came under the control of large business concerns, the whole price structure became cockeyed.

When I visited Europe, for example, I found that fruit was extremely expensive in Vienna, Austria. When I asked about this, I was told that the Italian farmers were refusing to grow fruit, so the price was high for what little fruit was available. The next day, when I went on to Italy, I saw a bulldozer destroying beautiful peach trees in an orchard south of Milan. When I asked the farmer why he was doing that, he said the people in Austria would not buy the fruit. The reason, of course, was that the price was too high in Vienna, causing demand to fall and the price paid to the Italian orchardist to drop. The farmer said he was following the orders of the local agricultural cooperative to 'limit production,' and so he was taking out his orchard.

The same day, a French newspaper published a photograph of French farmers, at the border with

Italy, overturning five or six trucks loaded with grapes in order to prevent their importation. Consumers in the French cities at the time were buying imported fruit and wine at high prices, undercutting their own farmers' understandable concern about the low prices they were getting for their produce.

This sort of thing happens because the commercial firms that stand in the position of middlemen can manipulate prices according to the information they release. If they tell consumers that prices are high because the supply of fruit is low, and tell the producers that sales are poor, then everything goes well for the middleman broker because he has control over the cash flow. Under this system no one knows the truth. Those businessmen and financiers who know and control information about the true production and cost figures determine the prices, always to their own advantage.

I call this the money-sucking octopus economy. At the center are politicians and the military-industrial-government complex (the heart of the octopus), who have centralized authority. The octopus's eight legs are the means to serve that center, which are: (1) maintenance of the transportation network, including road, rail, and air transportation; (2) control of agencies administering transportation; (3) supervision of communications; (4) establishment of an economic information network; (5) education and administrative advising; (6) control of financial institutions; (7) control of information; and (8) control of citizens' personal computers and registration.

Everything is pulled to the center with these eight legs. Although this action is carried out under the name of stimulating the regional economy of outlying areas, or maintaining regional culture, the wealth eventually accumulates in the center. The towel the octopus has tied around its head, like a sushi maker, is a ring of money, and this money, like a magnet, draws more money through its eight legs. Money attracts more money, and it goes on and on.

And what is this wealth being used for? It is used for establishing more centralized authority and strengthening armaments – more fuel for the gut of the octopus. This will lead to national enrichment and military strength – which, if allowed to escalate unchecked, results in the mad ambition to control the world. But pride goes before a fall, and in the end the octopus will either be hauled up by the master fisherman or will eat its own legs to spite itself.

This tragic dance of the money-sucking octopus is performed on the backs of the common people and the farmers. In the end, the octopus, with its legs waving wildly in every direction, is nothing more than the human comedy.

This reminds me of the time I visited Lumbini, Nepal, the birthplace of Sakyamuni Buddha. As I rested in the thick morning mist beneath a ficus tree, some local farmers appeared in twos and threes, and walked around the pond in front of me. They were turning prayer wheels and chanting, and then they disappeared. Time stopped for me. In that moment, I thought I heard the voice of the Buddha.

On my journey home that day, a person involved with maintaining sacred Buddhist sites showed me a proposal made by a Japanese architect for turning that place into a tourist spot. I was shocked. The plan was to connect the pond with a series of canals so people could worship from pleasure boats. In the center of the park, models of the great temples, churches, and shrines of the world would be built and used as hotels.

The idea was to make visiting sacred sites more convenient, shortening the time required to grasp the mind of the Buddha. Do I even have to say that it is impossible to capture the true form of the Buddha with religious theme parks and revolving lanterns?

Although the government prides itself on the fact that Japan has become an economic power, and a majority of the people consider themselves to be members of the middle class, everyone there can sense that the current prosperity and an upcoming economic crisis are sitting back-to-back.

Not long ago, more than 80 percent of the Japanese people were farmers, and only a small fraction of the people were in trades or industrial production. Now it is reversed. The primary farming industries account for barely 5 percent of the population, and even the secondary trade and manufacturing industries have been surpassed by the tertiary consumer service industries. If a typhoon of economic depression should arise, this structure will certainly collapse.

The same agrarian landscape that could be seen in Japan until just recently still exists in the farming villages of many parts of Asia, Africa, and India. In fact, one of the most common farming tools still used in many Indian villages today is the water buffalo cart. I sensed great pride in the words of a farmer who boasted to me that the design of this cart had not been changed or improved upon in the last three thousand years.

At the foundation of the so-called underdeveloped countries is a proud agrarian ethic. If these local economies were to imitate the developed countries, with their model of concentrated power and resources, the common people would be demeaned even as the country's profiteers temporarily prospered. These dignified farmers I have met see the skyscrapers of the developed nations as the tombstones of the human race. I am reminded of a Thai folksong that goes:

There is rice in the fields
There are fish in the water
The peddler shouts his wares
You can buy what you want
We have sown the seeds
Hurry, give them water
If you don't, they will die
Tonight the moon is full.

This song celebrates the belief that the greatest joy may be found among the farmers living with only the bare essentials.

The Illusion of the Law of Causality

Natural scientists have found that if you chill a cup of water, it will turn to ice, and if you heat the ice, it will turn back into the water. In the repetition of such experiments, they have seen that there is a cause and a result in the changes of matter.

When seawater is heated by the sun, it turns to vapor, rises in the sky to form clouds, turns to rain, falls on the earth, flows down in streams and rivers, and returns to the sea. With this cycle, meteorologists discern the cause of rain and clouds and think they have grasped the true nature of the water. But they do not understand the fundamental cause that explains *why* there is water on the earth and why clouds float in the sky.

When natural scientists set up measures to counter desertification, they begin by investigating its causes and the apparent results. They conduct studies of the desert environment, the climate, the soil, and the ecology of the living organisms. Then they create a plan for reforestation. In other words, as with Western medicine, they devise a swift, localized treatment of the symptoms. But the causes they base their solutions upon are not the fundamental causes. Their countermeasures serve not to heal, but rather magnify the scope of the problem.

Let me talk for a moment about my own experience with the pine forests in Japan. Lovely green pine trees growing near white sandy beaches have long been a representative landscape of the Japanese islands, but in the mid-1970s the pine trees began dying left and right. In a short time, the beautiful pines covering the hills have all but disappeared in many parts of Japan. The Regional Office of Forestry determined that the source of the damage was a nematode carried by a long-horned beetle. During the past ten years they have conducted widespread aerial chemical spraying in an attempt to exterminate the beetle.

My own village is in an area of red pine forests that

nourishes the matsutake mushroom, a mycorrhizal fungus highly prized for its flavor when cooked. I was unable to sit by and watch as the large green trees around my farm suddenly died, one after the other. Also, I had my doubts about the way in which the Office of Forestry had determined that the beetle and the nematode were the cause, so I put my past experience in plant pathology to use and spent more than three years doing research in one of my hillside huts.

The Office of Forestry's theory was that when the beetles laid their eggs in the tops of the pines, the nematodes living in association with the beetles invaded the pines, entered the tree's vascular system, and multiplied, blocking the passage of water and nutrients within the trunk and branches. This was said to cause the pines to suddenly wither and die. My experiments, however, showed a completely different result.

First of all, healthy pines are not likely to die, even when inoculated with nematodes. Second, I did not find the filamentous fungi that feed the nematodes (according to the Office of Forestry, nonspecific blue and black molds) present in the trunks of healthy pines, and the nematodes cannot live on pine sap alone. Then, when I studied the trunks of pines that had begun to show signs of dying, I discovered three or four *different* types of pathogenic fungi (*eumycetes*) that had not even been mentioned. These organisms are thought to have been introduced with imported lumber. But even when I inoculated pines with the hyphae that these fungi produced, they had little effect on the overall health of the tree.

Most fascinating from my research was the discovery that the pines first showed physiological abnormalities only after the mycorrhizal matsutake fungi were no longer present. The pine and matsutake fungi have a symbiotic relationship. The matsutake penetrates and breaks down the minerals in the soil, absorbing minute amounts of their nutrients, which it then supplies to the pine. In other words, the decline of the pine trees and the sudden decline in the matsutake fungus, which is occurring throughout Japan, seemed to be directly related.

What has given rise to the change among the communities of microorganisms in the soil of the pine forests in Japan? It is widely known that the soil of the pine forests is becoming more and more acidic, and that alone may account for the changes among the microorganisms. I believe that acid rain is the source of the acidity, but I cannot say so with certainty.

I have not yet reached a conclusion, but in relation to the cause, the results of my research point in an entirely different direction than does the theory of the Office of Forestry. The source of the problem is not a troublesome nematode, but rather that the matsutake fungi are dying, and as a result the pines have grown weak. Filamentous fungi have invaded their trunks, and finally, nematodes that feed on those fungi have invaded the pines. The nematodes and beetles are not the original culprits. They are doing nothing more than clearing away the corpses of the dead and dying trees. At the very least, they are only accessories to the crime, while the ringleader lies underground. But even if my theory is correct, if smog and acid rain turn out to be the source of the problem, then we are nearly back where we started from.

Of course, this research was done in my crude hut in the hills, so there is room for error, but the point is, what the world sees as cause and effect can be deceptive. Although I speak of the cycle of cause and effect, no one *really* knows what is happening. Still, the Office of Forestry goes out and sprays insecticide all over the forests. Who knows what unforeseen and potentially more serious environmental disaster that may lead to?

The Current Approach of Desertification Countermeasures

When people see that rain does not fall and there is no water in the desert, the first thing they think of is to build a dam to store river water. Then they build waterways and irrigation canals. They think that in order to use water efficiently, it is best to make straight waterways so that the water will flow faster. The Aswan Dam on the Nile has already been built and soon there will be similar large dams on the Yellow River in China, and the Narmada River in India. These may serve as expedient, short-term measures, but they will turn into long-range hundred-year mistakes.

The main reason water is disappearing from the rivers is that rain has stopped falling. The first step we must take in countering desertification is not to redirect the flow of rivers, but to cause rain to fall again. This involves revegetation.

Trying to revegetate the deserts by using the scarce water remaining in the rivers is putting the cart before the horse. No, we must first revegetate vast stretches of desert at one time, thereby causing rain clouds to rise from the earth.

There is now a plan to construct more than two hundred dams along the course of the Narmada River, the second holiest river in India after the Ganges. But when the dammed waters rise, it will submerge the forests, destroying the livelihoods of the people who live there, and millions will be driven to the deserts surrounding the river. This influx of people will put greater pressure on scant desert resources, and with the loss of the forests, the deserts will grow even larger.

The Indian government needs to decide whether it is better to carry out their hundred-year national plan of building hydroelectric power plants, or to revegetate the desert and bring the earth back to life.

It is also important to note that even if there are no rivers on the surface of the desert, there is water below the surface. In Saudi Arabia and in the desert area east of the Rocky Mountains in North America, water is pumped from aquifers hundreds of feet below the earth's surface. In the United States, the water is pumped to pivot farms, where it is dispersed by enormous sprinklers that form circles up to half a mile in diameter. Seeing the green circles these farms make in the desert, one can see the power of modern technology. But what will happen when these sprinklers have pumped all the remaining underground water that has been filtering down from the forests of the Rocky Mountains and collecting for tens of thousands of years?

When water is scarce, people think about economizing. With drip irrigation, plastic pipes are laid in the desert in an effort to use the least amount of water to the greatest effect. A Japanese university has been carrying out experiments using this sort of irrigation in Mexico, and it has been employed in Israel for some time. Of course, this method is effective as a localized remedy, but in view of the overall materials and energy needed, it is questionable whether or not drip irrigation can be adopted as a practical, long-term solution.

One experiment being carried out in Egypt plows super-absorbent resins into the soil to increase its ability to retain water. Other experiments focus on various types of water-retaining materials to use in place of humus, but these measures are also short-term expedients.

In China, the government has begun a massive effort to halt the expansion of China's great Taklamakan Desert. As in Sudan and Tanzania, they are using satellites and airplanes to conduct remote surveys of the current scale of desertification. They analyze underground water, soil salinity, and other conditions by boring holes to great depths, quantifying the results, making computer simulations, and testing the tolerance of plants raised in the harsh desert environment. But every plan for revegetation created in this way has failed. Then the governments in charge of the studies say they need to go back and reanalyze the data – which will, of course, cost more time and money.

Sure, you can create excellent fields in an arid area if you pump water from underground and sprinkle it on the desert, as they do on American pivot farms. But because irrigation water that has been applied in this way quickly evaporates, the salt is precipitated out, and builds up in the surface layers of the soil. To prevent this salinization, the salts from the irrigation water are drained into rivers or nearby 'dump sites,' causing toxic conditions there instead.

Methods such as those used in Saudi Arabia, Israel, and other places of filtering seawater with a synthetic resin membrane, removing the salt to turn the seawater into fresh water, circulating it, and thus creating farms in the middle of the desert, are also nothing more than short-term measures that require tremendous amounts of energy.

Some people think that to increase the vegetation on earth, it is best to plant trees that mature quickly. Today various types of fast-growing trees such as eucalyptus are being planted all over the world. These trees, however, typically require a lot of water when they are young, so a strenuous effort would have to be made to water the trees properly. When trees are watered only to a shallow depth, the soil becomes compacted. Then the water cannot percolate deeply into the ground, roots cannot extend, and in the end you might as well have poured water on heated rocks. For this reason many of the trees wither and die.

Desertification caused by sheep, cows, and goats is

also a serious problem. Not only do they eat the sparse vegetation, but they also eat the trees that people plant with the goal of restoration. It appears that we must decide how to control the number of domestic animals and how to give them proper management – a system that encourages healing and regenerating the soil upon which they graze – at the same time that we deal with the problem of the world's human population.

When they see that the food supply is insufficient, people hurry to cut down trees and try to grow crops as quickly as possible, often in burnt-over fields. Overall, however, vegetation is decreasing faster than it is regenerating, and desertification proceeds at an accelerating rate.

Scientific revegetation measures often consider only one route to healing the desert. As it is now, the various scattered, localized efforts to halt desertification end up as half-baked measures administered by government officials. The problem is that the water, soil, and plants are considered separately, with each being advanced by a separate department. A permanent solution will never come about in this way.

For the past fifty years or so, I have grown crops without tilling the soil and without using fertilizers or agricultural chemicals. I have done practically nothing, and the soil in my fields has become the best in my village. I simply scattered seeds in clay pellets, covered them with straw, and grew a healthy ground cover including white clover and vetch. I supplied nature with the tools, and then I relied on nature's disposition toward fertility. Although the climate and other conditions are different, I believe that this basic method will also work in revegetating the deserts.

Revegetating the Earth Through Natural Methods

When the director of the Desertification Prevention Council at the United Nations told me that he thought my natural farming methods could be useful in preventing the spread of the deserts, I was surprised. Looking back, though, I realize that the techniques I developed over those many years in Japan *could*, in fact, be used effectively to counteract desertification.

People have been living on the site of my natural farm since the Stone Age, and in ancient times the area was covered with an ancient forest of at least eight species of *Metasequoia*. It is said to have been a center of local culture about a thousand years ago. The area could be compared to the Silk Road in the way the culture flourished until the earth was eventually worn down, and the vibrant culture with it. The soil of this once fertile forestland eventually eroded down to the clay subsoil.

Years ago, at the site of my natural farm, people

tried planting mandarin orange trees, but the trees did not thrive, so they largely abandoned the land. That is the land I started with. Since then I have turned the soil of my family's orchard into soil as fertile as the forest soil it once was.

When I returned to my father's farm after the war, the trees in the citrus orchard were struggling. There was little vegetation on the surface, and the ground had become compacted. At first I thought the soil would improve quickly if I brought ferns and rotting tree trunks I found in the forest and buried them, but the experiment was a failure, mainly because it took too much work to bury enough material to make a significant difference. That organic farming technique might have eventually helped improve the soil, but it required a lot of labor for very little result. Like many other farming techniques, this was one that resulted in a net loss.

The start of my 'do-nothing' farming method came when I decided to simply plant a haphazard mixture of fruit trees, vegetables, grains, and clover among the acacia trees growing on the hillside and then observed which plants thrived and how they got along with one another. I neither cleared the land nor tilled it, and I used no fertilizers, herbicides, or pesticides. Now, some forty-five years later, it has turned into a fruit tree jungle. I believe that the techniques I have perfected after all these years can also be applied to regreening the deserts.

And so, while my journeys in later life have been inspired by my dream of revegetating the desert, unlike the typical scientist I have not tried to amass data or systematically formulate measures for preventing desertification. Instead, my desert prevention measures are strictly intuitive and based on observation. I arrived at them by using a deductive method. In other words, I started with the recognition that the causes of desertification in most areas are misguided human knowledge and action. If we eliminated them, I believed that nature would certainly heal itself.

Unfortunately, there are some places where the devastation is so bad that nature will have a difficult time recovering on its own – it lacks even the seeds that would form the basis of its recovery. The only work for people to do in such places is to gather the seeds and microorganisms nature needs and sow them there.

A good example is the natural farm of Ms. Aveliw, a woman who works for the Magsaysay Foundation in the Philippines. She read *The One-Straw Revolution*, did practical research and observation on her property for almost ten years, then set up her natural farm in four years mainly by scattering seeds and planting trees. She has created a true paradise. There is an assortment of fruit trees such as banana, papaya, guava, and durian, and some coffee trees. Beneath them is a thick ground cover of perennials and green manure. Orchids bloom everywhere, birds fly about, and fish swim in the ponds.

The soil of the Philippine islands is rather poor, and, as a result of reckless deforestation, you cannot find anything like a true tropical rain forest anywhere. So how was she able to develop this abundant jungle of fruit trees in so few years? The secret element was the harmony that existed between Ms. Aveliw and nature.

If we list the things necessary for plants to grow, then sunlight, nutrients, water, and air are sufficient to create a paradise. All the elements are created by nature itself. Even without instruments, nature is capable of performing a splendid symphony.

If you believe in intuitive insight, the road will open on its own accord. If you believe that the Philippines were originally a paradise, and sow seeds there, nature will create a forest of abundance and beauty. I was deeply moved by Ms. Aveliw's example.

Creating Greenbelts

My measures for revegetating the desert are essentially the same as the ones I used in establishing my natural farm. The fundamental concept of a natural farm, as I have described, begins with intuitively grasping nature's original form, where many varieties of plants and animals live together as a harmonious whole, joyfully and in mutual benefit.

As explained earlier, in the desert there are many places with rivers and underground water. One method for beginning a natural farming project in the desert is to revegetate the banks of the rivers and then gradually work outward from there to make the interior areas green. If we establish trees and other vegetation along the rivers, their range will naturally expand. If possible, however, we should scatter every kind of seed over the entire area at the same time and revegetate the desert all at once.

The theoretical basis of revegetation from the riverbanks follows the 'plant-based irrigation method.' It does not rely on running the river water through concrete waterways, but encourages the water to follow greenbelts of plants. It achieves non-irrigation agriculture by increasing water retention in the soil and the plants themselves.

Water naturally moves to lower areas, is carried by the roots of plants, and creeps toward dry areas. At the river's edge, reeds and cattails will flourish, and arundo grass (*Arundo donax*) will grow in clumps, protecting the banks. Pussy willows, purple willows, and alders will provide protection from the wind, cool the under story, and draw water.

If we plant every kind of plant, starting from the area around the river, the underground water will filter up the roots of the plants, and gradually a protective forest will develop. This is what I call plant-based irrigation.

For example, if you plant acacia trees sixty feet apart, in five or six years the trees will reach a height of thirty feet and the roots will have spread at least thirty feet in every direction, carrying the water with them. As the soil fertility increases and humus accumulates, the soil's ability to retain water will increase. Although the movement of underground water is slow, gradually it will move from one tree to the next, and they will act as water bearers.

If we were to apply this method for revegetating the desert, we would begin by planting woods along the rivers in the desert. Then, at right angles to the river, we would create greenbelts of natural forest instead of irrigation canals, and have them serve the role of waterways. In the center of these greenbelts, we would plant fruit trees and vegetables, creating natural farms. In this way, we would be creating food and rehabilitating the desert ecosystem at the same time.

You may think it reckless for me to say that we can revegetate the desert. Although I have confirmed this theory in my own mind and in my orchard and fields in Japan, I have had few opportunities to prove it on a large scale. Recently, however, the government of India asked me for technical assistance in carrying out an aerial seeding effort. I told them, in general, it is best to leave nature to nature, and let nature recover on its own. Sometimes, however, as in this case, if the land has been too badly damaged, we must provide nature with the materials it needs to become healthy again. I agreed to help with their efforts.

In India, there are more than five hundred varieties of trees that bear edible nuts and more than five hundred varieties of fruit trees. In addition to these, we should sow the seeds of five hundred varieties of grains, vegetables, and green manure, ideally on the barren Deccan Plateau and in the desert. No matter how bad the conditions are, some varieties will be suited to that place and will germinate, even if some die. These 'pilot' plants will help create conditions that will allow other plants to follow.

A second purpose in sowing a variety of plants and microorganisms is to awaken the sleeping earth. There are some deserts, particularly the sandy ones that have apparently lost their ability to support life and have all but died. Many savannas, however, exist in relatively young, clay soil. These deserts contain all the nutrients plants need, but for various reasons these nutrients are unavailable to them. In order to make these nutrients available, to rouse the earth, a variety of ground cover plants and microorganisms are necessary.

The earth will not come back to life if we only plant a small variety of trees we deem to be useful. A tree cannot grow up in isolation. We need to grow tall trees, midsized trees, shrubs, and understory plants all together. Once a mixed ecosystem is re-created, the rain will begin to fall again.

It seems logical for people to choose something special from nature and use it for the benefit of human beings, but when they do this, they make a big mistake. Taking one element from nature, in the name of creating something valuable economically (cash crops, for example), gives that element special value. It also implies that other elements have a lesser value. When human beings plant only 'useful' trees with high cash value in the desert, and cut down the undergrowth referring to those plants as 'weeds,' many plant species are lost. Often they are the very plants that are enriching and holding the soil together.

There is no good or bad among the life-forms on

earth. Each has its role, is necessary, and has equal value. This idea may seem simplistic and unscientific, but it is the basis for my plan to regenerate landscapes all over the world.

Appendix

Creating a Natural Farm in
Temperate and Subtropical Zones

When starting a natural farm, the first question you might ask is where it should be located and how you will choose the place to live on it.

You could go into a mountain forest and live in splendid isolation, if you like that sort of thing, but usually it is better to make a farm in the mountain foothills. The climate is better in an area that is slightly elevated from the valley floor; there is also less chance of flooding. It is easy to obtain firewood, grow vegetables, and find the other materials needed for satisfying the necessities of food, clothing, and shelter. If there is a river nearby, crops will be easier to grow, and you can establish a satisfying life for yourself.

No matter what the land is like, you can grow crops if you make the effort, but it is easier if the place is rich with the bounties of nature. It is ideal to find a place where large trees grow densely on the hills, the soil is deep and black or dark brown in color, and clean water is available. The natural farm should include not only fields but also the surrounding hills and forests. A good environment and fine scenery are wonderful elements for living an enjoyable life, both materially and spiritually.

Natural Protective Forests

The foundation for achieving success is to build deep, fertile soil. Here are some methods for achieving this.

1. Burying coarse organic matter such as decaying tree trunks and branches in the ground is one way, but this requires a great deal of labor. In general it is better to let plants do the work for you.
2. Plant trees, shrubs, grasses, and legumes with extensive root systems. These roots will soften the soil and bring nutrients from the lower levels back up to the surface, gradually improving it.
3. Cause rainwater to flow over the farm from the wooded slopes above. This water will

carry nutrients from the humus-rich forest soil. The essential thing is to maintain a continuous supply of organic material that is produced on the farm itself. This forms the basis of fertility for the entire system.

You can improve the protective forests on the slopes above the farm, but if there are no forested hills, new woods or bamboo thickets should be created. When creating or improving the protective forest, you should plant a mixture of trees, shrubs, and ground cover plants that are useful for several purposes. For example, they may be useful as a source of fuel and building materials, for providing habitat for birds and insects, and for producing food for farm animals, wildlife, and people. It is also good to include plants that have medicinal benefits, attract insects, and improve the soil. Often one plant fulfills many of these functions. The idea is to have all of the elements on the farm working together as one.

Raising a Protective Forest

The soil at the summit of a hill or on the ridgeline of mountains is often thin and dry leaving the hill bare at the top. In places like this, we should first grow trailing plants like *Ixeris debilis* and kudzu (*Pueraria lobata*) to halt the erosion of soil and then plant or sow the seeds of pines and Sawara cypress (*Chamaecyparis pisifera*), turning it into an evergreen forest. At first, fast-growing grasses such as eulalia (*Miscanthus sinensis*) and cogon grass (*Imperata cylindrica*), ferns such as bracken (*Pteridium aquilinum*) and scrambling fern (*Diplopterygium spp.*), and bushes such as bush clover (*Lespedeza spp.*), *Eurya japonica*, and cypress will grow densely. Gradually, as the soil improves, these plants will be replaced by a succession of other plants. Eventually, miscellaneous trees will begin to grow here and there from seeds deposited by the plants themselves, and by animals, birds, and the wind.

On the side of the hill, it is good to plant evergreens such as hinoki cypress (*Chamaecyparis obtusa*) and camphor, along with a mixture of other trees such as Chinese nettle tree (*Celtis sinensis*), Japanese zelkova (*Zelkova serrata*), paulownia (*Paulownia tomentosa*), cherry, maple, and eucalyptus. The foothills and the valley floor usually have deeper, more fertile soil, so you can plant trees such as walnuts and ginkgo among evergreens such as Japanese cedar (*Cryptomeria japonica*) and oak trees.

Bamboo groves are also useful in protective forests. Bamboo grows to full height from shoots in a single year. Its volume of growth is greater than that of the typical woody tree, so it is quite valuable as a source of coarse organic material when buried.

The shoots of Moso bamboo (*Phyllostachys edulis*) and other bamboos are edible. When dried, the stalks are light and easy to carry. Bamboo decomposes slowly when buried, so it is very effective for holding water and air in the soil. The organic matter produced as a result of its decomposition is wonderful for improving the structure of the soil.

Windbreaks

Trees planted as windbreaks are valuable not only for preventing wind damage but also for maintaining the fertility of the soil, filtering water runoff, and generally improving the environment for all creatures. Varieties that mature rapidly are Japanese cedar, hinoki cypress, acacia, and camphor. Camellia, parasol fir (*Firmiana simplex*), strawberry tree (*Arbutus unedo*), and star anise (*Illicium verum*), while slow growing, are also exceedingly beneficial. Depending on conditions, you may also be able to use trees such as evergreen oak, Japanese cleyera (*Ternstroemia japonica*), and holly.

Creating an Orchard

To create a natural orchard, take the same approach you would in planting trees in the forest. Cut trees in stages, taking nothing from the fields – that means the large trunks, branches, and leaves are all left to decay in their own time. These trimmings can be piled up along the contour lines of slopes to serve as improvised terraces.

The idea is to create a mixed orchard without clearing the land, only thinning. These days when land is cleared for an orchard, it is usually done with a bulldozer. The uneven surfaces of the slopes are flattened and roads are created to facilitate mechanized management.

Using machinery to create roads in the orchard makes it easier to apply fertilizer and other agricultural chemicals, but this is not necessary with the natural method. The only heavy labor is picking the fruit, and that is done by hand. I believe that success is actually more likely if you have little money when beginning the orchard. That way you introduce neither machines nor capital.

The leaves and branches of trees that were cleared and left on the ground, along with the tree roots, will slowly decay, becoming a long-term source of organic fertilizer. They will provide nutrients for the fruit trees for about as long as it takes the young orchard trees to grow to the size of the woodland trees that were thinned.

Furthermore, the organic matter provides a welcoming environment for ground cover to grow. The ground cover helps to suppress weeds, prevents soil erosion, stimulates the soil microorganisms, and improves the soil's structure and overall vigor.

Just like trees planted in a forest, the fruit trees are best planted along the contour of the slope. If possible, you should dig holes for planting, add coarse organic matter, and then plant the trees in a raised mound on top of that. Trees that are planted and grown in a natural way live longer and are more resistant to insects and disease than those grown with extra fertilizer and agricultural chemicals.

One of the problems with using a bulldozer to create an orchard is that when you flatten the land, you scrape off the topsoil. The topsoil contains the majority of the organic matter that has accumulated for many years. A farm cleared by a bulldozer and left untouched for ten years dries out and loses soil to erosion; its economic value is greatly reduced. Another problem with conventional clearing is that the trees are clear-cut and burned. At a single stroke, the fertility of the soil is diminished for decades.

In about twelve inches of topsoil, there are enough nutrients to sustain an orchard for ten years without adding fertilizer. If you have three feet of rich earth, the orchard can be sustained for approximately thirty years. If we can retain and maintain the richness of natural forest soil by using a soil-building combination of plants, including nitrogen-fixing plants such as white clover, beans, and vetch, then no-fertilizer cultivation is possible indefinitely.

Creating 'Fields' in the Orchard

Usually a 'field' means a place devoted exclusively to growing crops, but the spaces between the fruit trees in an orchard can also be considered a field. The system and methods of cultivation, however, differ greatly depending on whether the orchard or conventional flat fields predominate. Making a field where fruit trees are the primary crop and grains and vegetables are grown between the trees is almost exactly the same as creating an orchard for natural farming. It is not necessary to clear the land, and there is no need to carefully prepare the ground or bury coarse organic matter.

In the first stage of making the orchard field, we need to control weeds and bring the soil to maturity.

It is good to start by sowing the crops among green manure plants and buckwheat during the first summer, and radishes and mustard during the first winter. In the next year you can plant strong twining plants that reproduce well without fertilizer, such as adzuki beans and cowpeas (black-eyed peas) in summer, and hairy vetch in winter. These twining plants, however, can cover up vegetables and fruit tree seedlings, so they must be tended from time to time. As the field matures, you can grow a wide variety of other crops.

Creating a Conventional Field

Most lowland field crops are annuals that are produced in just a few months to half a year. These are the typical garden vegetables. The ones that reach about two or three feet in height, like tomatoes, eggplant, and peppers, have shallow roots and are a bit temperamental because of their long history of hybridization. Because the time between sowing and harvesting fast low-growing crops such as radish, lettuce, and garden turnips is short, and several crops are typically grown in one year, the surface of the ground is exposed to the elements for much of the growing season. We must accept the fact that some soil loss will occur in these fields because of rain, and that the soil will lose some of its vitality during droughts and cold weather. These problems can be minimized, however, by keeping the soil covered with mulch and by growing a continuous ground cover.

When creating the field, the most important concern is preventing soil erosion. If the land is sloped, it should be terraced to make the surface level or close to level. This can be accomplished by building up earthen banks or making stone walls, then creating the terraced fields. The success or failure of this work depends on knowing the type of soil so the banks will not crumble. For the stone walls, it is ideal to use the stones dug up from the field or hillside itself.

Creating Paddy Fields

Of course, it is easy to make paddy fields by clearing the plains with bulldozers, carrying away the vegetation, and leveling the ground. This also makes it possible to increase the size of the fields, making mechanized agricultural more convenient.

There are many disadvantages to this method, however. (1) The topsoil of the paddy is of uneven depth, resulting in uneven growth of crops. (2) Because the large, heavy machinery puts pressure on the soil, the soil becomes compacted. Groundwater will collect and stagnate. This creates anaerobic conditions, which cause the roots to decay, leading to damage from disease and insects. (3) When a field is created by using heavy machinery, the ridges around the fields become hard, the microorganisms in the soil change or die out, and the soil atrophies.

Trees are the guardians of the soil. Even in flooded paddies, growing large and small trees on mounds right in the fields themselves is an excellent idea. The paddies near Sukhothai, Thailand, are filled with such trees. Those fields are among the finest examples of the natural faming method for growing paddy rice anywhere in the world since they join the farmers with a diversity of plants and animals – including draft animals, fish, and amphibians – into a harmonious whole.

It is unnecessary to go to great lengths to grow rice in paddy fields, since it is quite possible to grow paddy rice in dry fields watered only by the rain. I have shown this in my fields in Japan. The main reason people grow rice in a flooded field is to control weeds. I take care of weeds by not plowing, spreading straw mulch, and growing white clover continuously on the surface of the soil. I get better results that way without doing much at all, and the soil improves with each passing year.